Bollywood

by Cathy West

Ransom

StarStruck

Bollywood

by Cathy West

Illustrated by Demitri Nezis

Published by Ransom Publishing Ltd.
Radley House, 8 St. Cross Road, Winchester, Hants. SO23 9HX
www.ransom.co.uk

ISBN   978 184167 054 6

First published in 2014

Bollywood

Contents

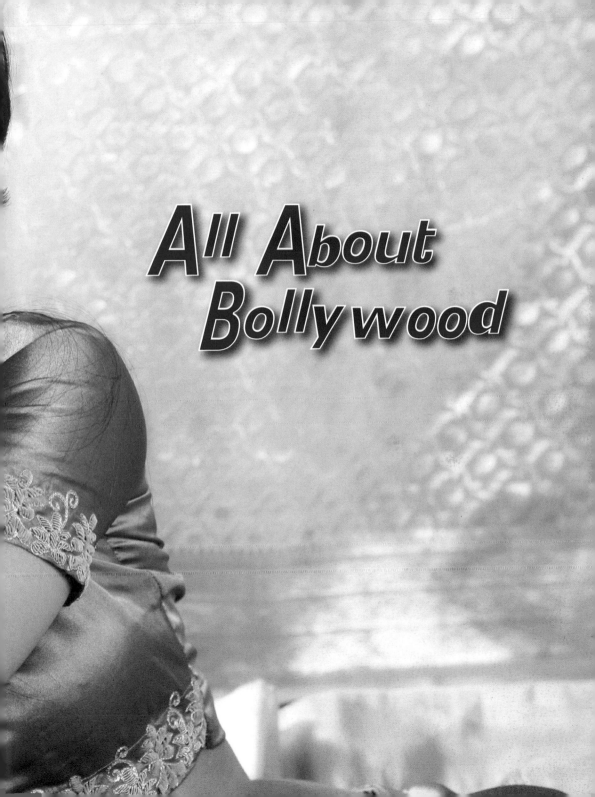

All About Bollywood

What is Bollywood?

Bollywood is the name for the films made in Mumbai in India.

In the past the city of Mumbai was called Bombay.

INDIA

Mumbai

Why is it called Bollywood?

In the 1970s India started making more films than Hollywood (in the USA).

So people mixed the words 'Bombay' and 'Hollywood' to make the name Bollywood.

Mumbai, India.

Now people all over the world see Bollywood films.

In 2002 people bought 3.6 billion tickets to see Bollywood movies. In the same year they bought 2.6 billion tickets for Hollywood movies.

Hollywood, USA.

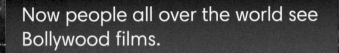

7

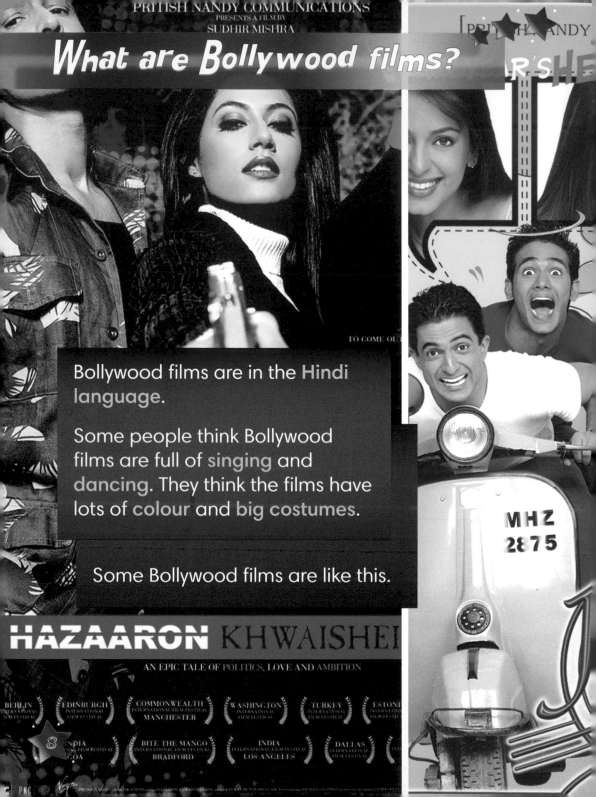

What are Bollywood films?

Bollywood films are in the Hindi language.

Some people think Bollywood films are full of singing and dancing. They think the films have lots of colour and big costumes.

Some Bollywood films are like this.

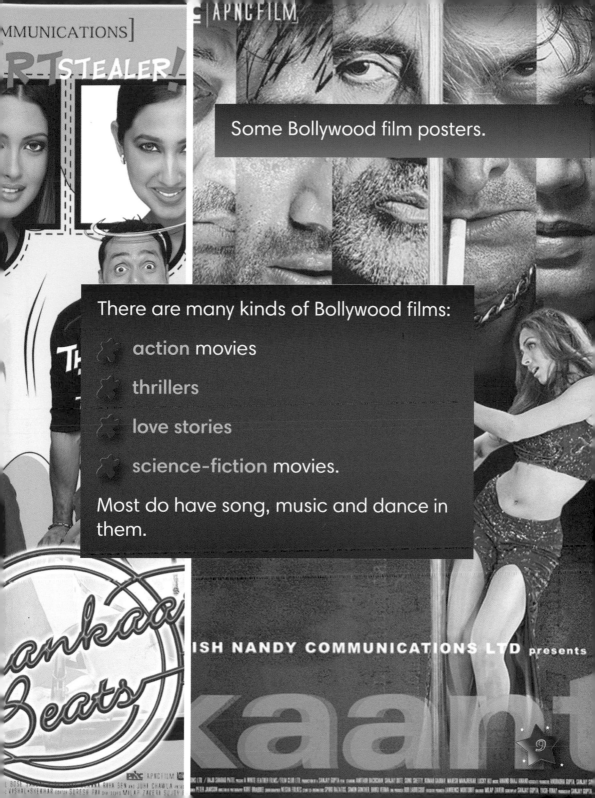

Some Bollywood film posters.

There are many kinds of Bollywood films:

- action movies
- thrillers
- love stories
- science-fiction movies.

Most do have song, music and dance in them.

Bollywood music

Bollywood films mix **music**, **singing** and **dance** into the story.

The songs must be good!

Top Bollywood **actors** are very good at acting and dancing.

Not many are good **singers**.

Sometimes a **different** person does the singing for the movie. The actor **pretends** to sing.

A. R. Rahman is a famous Bollywood composer. He mixes many different kinds of music.

Harshdeep Kaur is a famous Bollywood playback singer.

The people who sing are called playback singers. You hear them – but you never see them.

Some playback singers are very well known.

Some people go to a movie just to hear their favourite playback singer.

11

Bollywood dance

Most Bollywood films have dance in them.

The dance parts have a big **cast**: there are many actors. The music is always exciting.

Some films have an 'item song'.

This is a song by an actor who is only in the film to sing that song.

These actors are very good. People will go to the film just to see them sing.

Top actor **Mallika Sherawat** sings as an 'item girl' in Bollywood films.

12

The dancing is **arranged** by a **choreographer**. The choreographer decides the dance moves.

Some Bollywood choreographers are very famous.

Many Bollywood song and dance scenes are now filmed in **Switzerland**.

Top Bollywood actors

Amitabh Bachchan has acted in more than 180 films.

His first film was in 1971.

Deepika Padukone is a very popular actor.

Her first Bollywood film was **Om Shanti Om** in 2007.

Shilpa Shetty is an actor and a model. She has acted in nearly 40 films.

Shilpa has a younger sister, Shamita Shetty. Shamita is also a Bollywood film actor.

Aamir Kahn is an actor. He is also a writer, director and TV presenter.

He acted in his first film when he was aged 8. His most popular films are **Ghajini, 3 Idiots** and **Dhoom 3.**

Top Bollywood films

Dhoom 3

Stars: Aamir Khan, Katrina Kaif

Type of film: Action, thriller

Date: 2013

Money earned: US$ 93 million

Chennai Express

Stars: Shahrukh Khan, Deepika
                  Padukone

Type of film: Action, comedy

Date: 2013

Money earned: US$ 78 million

Krrish 3

Stars: Hrithik Roshan, Vivek Oberoi

Type of film: Superhero

Date: 2013

Money earned: Over US$ 51 million

Ek Tha Tiger

Stars:	Salman Khan, Katrina Kaif
Type of film:	Spy thriller
Date:	2012
Money earned:	US$ 59 million

3 Idiots

Stars:	Aamir Khan, Kareena Kapoor
Type of film:	Comedy drama
Date:	2009
Money earned:	US$ 66 million

Yeh Jawaani Hai Deewani

Stars:	Ranbir Kapoor, Deepika Padukone
Type of film:	Romantic comedy
Date:	2013
Money earned:	US$ 52 million

Chapter One

Star sister

Hansa's elder sister, Sabeena, had a part in a big Bollywood movie.

Hansa was helping Sabeena learn her lines.

Sabeena had to get all her dance steps right, too. She would be dancing alongside the star actress, Maya Ka Phool.

'You're so beautiful and talented. You should be the star,' Hansa told her sister.

Sabeena laughed. 'I wish!' she said with a grin.

'I wish I could be in a Bollywood movie, too,' Hansa said.

'You're a very good dancer,' said Sabeena. 'I think you could be.'

'But I'm so plain! Maybe if I were as beautiful as you,' Hansa said.

'I know! You act my part and I'll pretend to be Maya Ka Phool,' Sabeena said.

The two sisters had good fun acting the different roles in their front room.

Chapter Two

In the film studio

'Why don't you come to the film studio with me?' Sabeena said to her sister. 'You can see what it's really like to be in a movie.'

'Am I allowed?' Hansa asked, hopping from foot to foot in excitement.

Hansa had never been to a film studio before. She couldn't believe she was going to see the legendary star actress, Maya Ka Phool, for real.

At the film studio, Hansa was very excited. She was allowed to sit next to the film director.

They were filming the big dance number. Hansa thought Sabeena looked amazing. Maya Ka Phool was dancing with her male co-star, Salman Khan.

Suddenly, Maya bumped into Salman.

'Salman, you fool! You're doing it wrong,' Maya screeched.

'Cut! Cut!' yelled the director.

Chapter Three

Problems on the set

Hansa gasped. She had practised those dance steps with Sabeena. She knew it was Maya, not Salmon, who had gone the wrong way. The director knew it too.

'It's left, left, then right,' the director told Maya. He waved his finger at her.

Maya yelled at the director. 'I can't be expected to work in these conditions,' she said.

Then she stormed off the set.

All the cast stood and stared in amazement. How could they finish the movie without the main star?

But, the director didn't seem to care.

'You!'

He pointed his finger at Sabeena. 'You will play the star role.'

Sabeena was stunned.

'But … who will take my part?' Sabeena asked.

Chapter Four

'I can do it!'

'I can do it!' Hansa said to the director. 'I've practised all the lines and dance moves at home. I know them!'

The director looked Hansa up and down and tutted.

Hansa was afraid he would say she was too plain and boring to be in a Bollywood movie. Some of the other actresses whispered rudely behind their hands.

The director waved his hand at his assistants. Hansa was whisked away to the dressing room.

In the dressing room, Hansa was given a costume like the other dancing girls.

A make-up artist did her make-up. Then the assistants took her back to the film set.

Everyone gasped with surprise when they saw her.

'Wow! You look beautiful,' Sabeena said.

'And ... action!' the director called.

Everyone took their places.

Hansa was perfect. The movie was a big success.

Was this the start of a new career?

action movie	India
actor	item girl
arrange	item song
arranger	movie
Bollywood	Mumbai
Bombay	playback singer
cast	pretend
choreographer	romantic comedy
comedy	science-fiction
costume	singer
drama	spy thriller
film studio	Switzerland
Hindi language	thriller
Hollywood	